My daddy ... listens to me.

My daddy ... bakes cakes with me.

My daddy... watches football with me.

My daddy... takes me out in the car.

My daddy... takes me to dance class.

My daddy ... splashes in puddles with me.

My daddy... takes me swimming.

My daddy ... takes me shopping.

My daddy... makes me feel better when I am hurt.

My daddy ... changes my nappy.

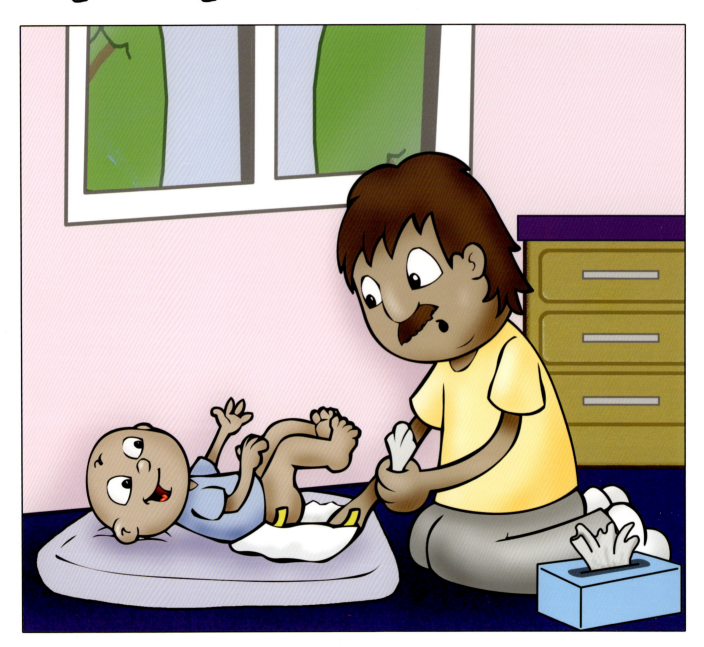

My daddy ... has dinner with me.

My daddy ... sings songs with me.

My daddy... takes me for walks.

My daddy... gives me a bath.

My daddy... reads stories to me.